DECIDUOUS

EXPRESSIONS OF FALLING IN LOVE, GRIEF, AND LIFE

Higherhawk

J JAF Publishing, LLC
Kansas City, Missouri

Dedicated to F.A.M.

Acknowledgements

Over three years ago I started this book and I was inspired by someone very special to, go for it and to never give up. Giving up seemed so easy at times, yet I never did. It has taken awhile, but here it is. I could have never made it this far without my family and their undying support. I am so grateful for them and their love.

Thank you Brian for always picking me up off the floor. The following people are those that have always been there for me and I am am eternally grateful for them: Ann, Jacquie, Ali, Amanda and John from Voella.com who helped me in so many ways, Mary McDonald and Mira, Jayne from One Lucky Pup, Jenny, Samantha, Jimmie, Bethy, Katie, Melly, Mel, Jaleekqua, Patty, and Jane. Peet's coffee for keeping me awake with their amazing coffee, The Savory Plum for giving me a place to express myself for so many hours.

Thank you so much to Lee Zimmerman for his inspirational artwork and for allowing me to showcase his brilliance in this book of poetry.

A special thank you to Raine Cooper for her inspiration and love.

Without Paris Andren this book would never have been realized. She is my best friend and mentor. Her countless hours of dedication and inspiration gave this project life. I will never be able to express my gratitude enough to her...I love you my dear friend.

Higherhawk~

"Of all the paths you take in life, make sure a few of them are dirt."

–John Muir

Contents

Love 1

Surface 3

Wild 4

Leaves 5

Ripe: Pen and Ink 6

Ripe 7

Jump 8

Doorway 9

She Carved: Pen and Ink 10

She Carved 11

Fairytale 12

Shelter 13

Spilling Over Me:
Pen and Ink 14

Spilling Over Me 15

Her Gift 16

Cradle 17

Eager To Taste:
Pen and Ink 18

Eager To Taste 19

Render 20

Purpose 21

Dew Drop 22

Wet Petal 23

Blanket Of Affection 24

Do You Know 25

Ocean: Pen and Ink 26

Ocean 27

Open Sea 28

I Feel You 29

Bronze 30

Waiting 31

My Heart Sinking 32

The Veil 33

Strike Gently: Pen and Ink 34

Strike Gently 35

Once Again 36

Streaming 37

Ribbons: Pen and Ink 38

Ribbons 39

Nestled 40

Moonlight Whispers 41

Eternal Muse 42

Against The Edges 43

Untouched 45

Reveal: Pen and Ink 46

Reveal 47

Clay 48

Clutches 49

Warm Current 50

Wilderness and
The Wolves 51

Warmest Breath 52

Your Ink 53

You 54

Virgin 55

Fracture: Pen and Ink 56

Fracture 57

The Poem 58

Grief 59

Blanket Of Fire 61

Crest 63

Slips Further: Pen and Ink 64

Slips Further 65

Half Moon 66

Centuries 67

A Whisper and A Scream 68

Collectively 69

Soft Core: Pen and Ink 70

Soft Core 71

Coupled 72

Candle 73

Grasping 74

Another Heart 75

My Own Spit 76

Burning 77

Droplets 79

Sonance: Pen and Ink 80

Sonance 81

Pieces 82

Dreams 83

Bare 84

Pluck 85

River 86

My Weakest Breath 87

Assumption 88

The Echo Of Her Need 89

Sadness 90

Held 91

Etched 92

Mira 93

Strangers 94

Freedom 95

Our Paths: Pen and Ink 96

Our Paths 97

Life 99

Clinch 101

Veins 102

Fury 103

Blindfold 104

Tongue 105

Canvas 106

Dry and Thirsty 107

Fingers: Pen and Ink 108

Fingers 109

Honor 110

Cage 111

Miracle: Pen and Ink 112

Miracle 113

We 114

Shortcut 115

Marrow 117

Protect 118

Together 119

Inspiration: Pen and Ink 120

Inspiration...121

Saltwater...122

Acorn 123

Dilate 124

Persuasion 125

Skin 126

Shore 127

Foundation 129

Beyond The Ache 131

Poet's Pain: Pen and Ink 132

Poet's Pain..133

PART ONE

Love

Surface

What lies beneath the surface of this romantic is something
        greater than words or the material of this world.
The seasons change quickly and the tides never rest.
The sun and shadows dance until the moonlight chases them
        away.
The wind mimics the sound of every heartbeat and the birds
        never stop flying.
The grass is warm and if you lie down, it wraps around you like
        a blanket.
You can scream as loud as you like and the echoes scream right
        back.
The rain tastes like wine and the lightning always makes you
        laugh.
You walk around barefoot and never stub your toes.
So please leave your frowns behind and your doubts at the door
        because what lies beneath the surface—is oh so much
        more.

Wild

My heart is too wild, it can't live without the raw...the true
    engagement of life and death.
Anything else is just the sunrise and sunset, the in-between
    that should never settle across my tongue.
I need the shooting stars to hold on to...do not ache, just caress
    the edges so I don't burn up too fast.

5

Leaves

We are but leaves carried where the wind wields us.
We choose to let go.
Or...
We cling tight to the edge of what whittles us slowly away.

Ripe: Pen and Ink

Ripe

She whispers softly to me...
Show me your heart again.
Let it be a pillow that I rest my head upon while your words
make love to me.
As our ripe flesh glistens in the morning sun let me get lost
in each word.
Lost in every beat as the fire still dances through my body
and my breath runs away.

8

Jump

Love is always there.
Hovering on the edge.
Waiting for you to save it from the fall, or take its hand and
jump.

Doorway

I have always felt the warmth against my fingers reaching for
the doorway to the love in my heart, yet I have never
had the courage to open it—until you.

She Carved: Pen and Ink

She Carved

She quickly caught his eye.
Drawing forth his pen as she slowly
stretched out her leg.
It began.
Her moves became his words.
Writing her body as every curve flexed before him.
Every step she took, his heart tried to keep pace.
He felt his breath fall away as her body explodes into the
    sunrise and the sunset.
She was serenading him with her flesh, as the stars would
    sparkle for the moon.
She carved every thought from inside his being.
When she came to a halt, he waited eagerly on the edge for
    her next step.
She was the next exhale he would set free.
She was every drop of ink dancing from his pen, forming
    words he never knew existed within his heart.

Fairytale

There is a fairytale in every flower.

Their color and texture carry so many moments, from the
first thrust of their bloom, to the slow wilt before
swaying into slumber, gently closing their eyes.

Each bloom carries a thousand kisses along with so many
tears.

They have touched the softest skin, delicately brushing
across moments where naked flesh sighs.

They have fluttered through the sunlight, raining over the
toes of barefoot lovers in secret gardens.

They have been held by countless fingers offering their
undying love, and buried with those that we can only
dream of.

They tell each tale screaming with lustful fragrances, of all
the past fairytales that live around us.

Shelter

Look down into the shelter of your palms.
That is where my heart resides.
Resting gently against everything you touch.
Every time you press your fingers to your bare breast,
I am brought closer to the edge of a love my heart longs to
    rest tenderly next to.

Spilling Over Me: Pen and Ink

Spilling Over Me

You, the one who carries my heart and holds my hand.
Come closer.
Pull me in.
Take each step with me as we begin to sway in the love we
    hold together.
The slightest embrace of your soft skin kissing mine sets me
    on fire.
Only to be fanned by a sudden breath from your heart,
    spilling over me with an unsuspecting urge to let go.
The touch of your tongue's edge like a razor—cuts me down.
My eyes giving in and giving you all of me, as I sink into the
    softest pool of silk, drowning in your every desire.

Her Gift

I felt myself fall breathless in the misty morning air.
Something about that moment held me silent, as if I no
    longer needed to breathe.
As if I needed to let that air touch me.
Gently brushing across my still lips, hushing what this heart
    wanted to spill.
Taming that fire before it could catch hold of what might
    have let it burn awhile longer.
So I let go...
I let that air make love to my fear forcing it to fall from my
    heart and lay gently within my soul.

Cradle

In these moments of pure love cradled in my hands I feel so
    many things.
So many feelings that I know you feel too, they ricochet
    throughout my heart bursting beyond my under
    standing.
So much joy and pain swirling into tears, that fall from the
    edge of memories and moments I have yet to live.
Oh the sway of each step I take walking the wire day by day
    and some days I just want to fall.
Then I feel your head rest on my shoulder, your warm
    breath dances across my neck, and I know you're there.
I feel you touch the love I tend in my hands.
Is it your heart I am holding between my fingers.
Are we holding it together...
In these moments that seem to bring me into the dizzy haze
    of my dreams and
I look love right in the eyes.
I feel so alone yet so close to you, please cradle my heart.
For I can't seem to hold both the joy and the pain that slips
    between my fingers.

Eager To Taste:
Pen and Ink

Eager To Taste

Fixated on the place nearest your heart.
Do you feel my breath caressing your breast.
A warm prelude to what has overrun my resistance.
Let me touch the most delicate part of your body.
These lips eager to taste love emitting through your skin,
quivering with every thrust of your breath.
Gasps fall like raindrops, drenching our flesh on fire...
Painting us in swirls of ecstasy.
Unleashing more than either of us dare to grasp...
Too lost in the fall.

Render

Don't say a word.
Your unaided heart says everything your eyes are trying to
    render unreal.
Tenderness tickled beyond resistance, leaving you exposed.
Transparent to my desire, wanting a touch of this bashful
    blooming, like a sunrise unable to see beyond the night.
Carrying your fresh fear seeping a belated ache still trying to
    hold its breath.

Purpose

Do not try so hard to exist sweet child.
Your colors are so unique.
Each flower, no matter how small or how long it blooms, has
a purpose in this world.

Dew Drop

Don't fall for her, fall with her.
Cradle her lips with yours, one petal touching the other with
such delicate embrace.
Erupting silently together, soaked in the first breath of sun
light, drowning in dew drop tears falling over your
naked desire, never letting go of one another.

Wet Petal

Wrap me up in the silence of your eyes.
Pull me into the naked whisper of your voice, gently follow
    ing the warmth of a breath relaying your heart's wish to
    ease my fear.
Release the pressure of so many tears waiting to fall.
Held beyond the light of day never knowing what it is to
    spill into the sunlight, never knowing where to fly.
Are you trying to save them from the sounds of an ache
    echoing only in my heart that once felt like the wind.
Are you hoping they would fall in joy and somehow ripple in
    the sunlight still reaching like fingers for what lay
    beneath my deepest desire.
I hope you see it, because I can't.
Even though I still feel it.
I feel it, like I feel every step I take.
Like every dream I have and every wish that slips from my
    tongue.
Oh I still feel it, like the wildflower bathing in morning dew.
Waiting for the sun to dry each wet petal, begging to share
    its fragrant exhale.

Blanket Of Affection

In your heart is where I will lay my weary head.
Each day I find it so easy to reach for your supple lips.
Like the sunrise thrusting into the blanket of night,
I will paint all the colors of my deepest affection across the
   sound of a new smile.
Never letting you fall anywhere except into the blinding
   light of unconditional love.

Do You Know

Do you even know the way you touch me.
Do you even know how you fill every thought I have.
Can you possibly know how you feed my flesh with every
    smile.
Like raindrops over new born flowers stretching their
    thirsty petals, drinking every drop hoping you will
    pluck me.
Take me to your garden where we can bathe in every sun
    rise.
Do you hear my breath vanish as you walk through me as
    gentle as sunlight showering through stained glass
    draping me in the colors of your fire.
I can't say a word even though my soul is screaming out
    your symphony.
You hold every word that exists within me.
They are born for you out of the ocean in your eyes.
Drifting in a gentle storm that I cannot help but willingly let
    draw me off course.
Pulling me closer.
Laying me over and over again across your delicate shore.

Ocean: Pen and Ink

27

Ocean

She sat watching the waves cling gently to the shore and
   then return to the deep blue.
Carrying away the tears fallen from the ocean in her heart.

Open Sea

There is a stillness that falters out in the open sea.
Something beyond the calm pulling at my soul, or is that
your echo calling me home.

I Feel You

I feel you everywhere swimming in the deepest part of me.
In every step I take, you take with me.
We share every breath taken in and released.
In every blink of my eyes, in every tear shed...I feel you.
I feel your lips as mine slowly grow across my face.
I forever feel your hand holding mine so tight.
As I lay and chase my dreams looking for you...
You are there.

Bronze

There is a woman in my life I have neglected.
She rests so still in peaceful hope of being touched once
  again...
Of feeling my fingers stroke her perfect and polished body
  that reflects my hidden heartbeat, a place riddled in
  memory, still holding so many chords waiting to be
  caressed.
Her long bronze neck stretched...in need of being set free.

Waiting

Often times the most gentle souls have the wildest hearts.
Yet in many cases they are waiting.
Waiting for someone or something to set them free.

My Heart Sinking

Maybe I should of tried to rescue my heart sinking on the
    shores of your soul.
Each wave crashing, rendering me helpless to the storm you
    inflict upon my fresh enduring flesh.
Yet strike my body, drown my senses, let me be the rock
    that your waves crash on continuously.
Sinking in all that you are and everything my body needs.

The Veil

Do you see the depths in her eyes.
What appears as fragility is merely the veil to a forest too
    wild to set free.
Where trees stand tall.
The wind is a welcome friend, stirring up the fragrance of
    her soul still innocent as a child.
Yet unafraid to dirty her shoes running deeper into the un
    touched grass of her imagination.

Strike Gently: Pen and Ink

Strike Gently

You found it amongst the shards scattered at the bottom of
  my fractured heart.
The last match laying in a pile of dreams.
Hanging on a prayer for the feel of your fingers taking hold
  of this wounded, yet still beating beacon.
I only ask that you strike gently on the edge of my soul
  before you set me on fire...
Lifting me out of the ashes.

Once Again

Play with my heart once again.
Find the fragile notes seeking the rhythm of your hands.
Bring my pulse into a song that only you can hear.
That only you know how to touch.

Streaming

Show me the light that lives beyond the setting sun.
Give me reason to believe in more than just the faint
　　starlight reflecting in my eyes...
As I wait to catch you streaming across the night sky.

Ribbons: Pen and Ink

Ribbons

She always smiled as she looked off into the sunset.
She knew that soon he would too.
And that they would share the same colors together.
Holding hands through the ribbons of a setting sun.

Nestled

Somedays you may not hear me whisper in your ear or
    touch your skin.
It is only because I am already nestled deep within your
    heart, fast asleep.

Moonlight Whispers

She took hold of me lying naked and dripping with moon
    light whispers,
Catching every tear with her fragile lips, tasting all the joy
    and sadness secreting from my dreams,
Promising never to let go.

Eternal Muse

Caught by the wind of her wings drifting over the path of
my tears, fanning my fears.
Carry me away my eternal muse.
Bring me back to your breast so I can nestle closer to your
heart.
Where you can run your fingers through my hair chasing
away every shadow lingering within my thoughts.
Let me become the breath never straying far from your lips.
Released slow, still wet with sensual thoughts, pressing
deeper against the warmth of our intentions, to never
leave this moment together.

Against The Edges

Hold me gently.
Press me naked against the edges of your voice.
Whisper away my weaknesses as my armor falls to the floor.
Like a warm breeze filled with sunlight, your breath pours
    from within your heart, showering my cold, crippled,
    and trembling soul with the light my body had bathed in
    once before.
A feeling similar to the first ray of sunshine at the dawn of
    spring,
Or the last time I felt your soft lips press gently into mine.
Hold this rough and bruised body until I can stand by your
    side again.

Untouched

Every breath she takes is poetry.
To be able to watch her body arch in such a serene gesture is
    a gift.
I can't even imagine the thought of the slightest exhale of
    laughter escaping from her lips without my heart
    pounding.
Her eyes touch me the way sunlight finds a cold morning
    slowly warming me from the first subtle graze of my
    flesh.
Her delicate skin seems to pour out before me like the wind
    so effortless and filled with the scent of an untouched
    flower waiting to be held.

Reveal: Pen and Ink

Reveal

Don't dress up.
I want to see you raw.
Show me your heart, not what you color it with.
Reveal to me the deepest part.
Naked, bare, drenched in sunlight, waiting to be touched...
I want to taste such essence.
I want your substance to spill over my lips and crawl closer
    to my heart.

Clay

Her skin, delicate like liquid silk pouring over my rough,
jagged edges.
Melting these bruised and broken corners covered with ache
into soft clay.
Waiting and wanting her fingers to press me into her desire.
Needing to be filled with a tenderness that once cried like
the sunrise being born from the darkness we found
each other in.
Reaching blindly one last time never knowing that the other
was there.
Yet you did, you held out your soft hand carving your way
into the deepest place of my heart.
Let me run between your fingers as you mold me into more
than I ever was.
Show me all that I can be in your delicate embrace and
everything you ever dreamed of my love.

Clutches

My heart hovers above the shadow, feeling so much cold air nipping at its downward feathers, pressing against the wind while my body stretches into the warm sunlight of freedom, never wanting to give into anything except the outright clutches of love's warm embrace.

Warm Current

Thank you for the sunlight you bring to my heart.
You don't realize how much you heal my ache.
My longing for the light that always seems to hide behind a
    shadow, you have now chased away.
You have taken hold of the soil in my soul sweet flower and
    you brought the sun with you.
Lets sway together in the warm current breathing across our
    faces covered with light from a new day.

Wilderness and The Wolves

I surrender.

I will follow the moonlight beyond the veil of my heart.

Like silent fingers caressing a song that my soul cannot
 resist.

Tempting me back through the fear you know I want to
 run from.

Fill me with the courage to take each step closer to the
 eternal embrace that I seek inside your arms.

Take my hand, let's run through the wilderness and the
 wolves without looking back.

The sunrise will find us before the darkness draws near.

Wrapping us within the dawn, still painted in starlight
 fading into the horizon.

52

Warmest Breath

Be still please...for just one moment more.
You are more than what the sunlight could dare to catch in
    it's warmest breath.
I drift over a rare moment truly visible to my heart.
Hoping never to lose focus of this miracle basking in the
    blink of these eyes, never wanting to shut or ever take
    the liberty to look away...for fear to lose the essence
    held in that moment in the sun that I so desperately
    want to hold for just one second more.

Your Ink

I love everything that crosses your mind.
That pours over your soft lips.
Brought to life by the tips of your fingers.
Unleashed by your pen, drowning me in the flow of your
    ink.

You

You found the courage lost from my heart.
You found the armor scattered about my soul.
You tended my every wound.
You brought me to my feet when fallen.
You caress every scar easing my pain as I rest safely in your
    arms.
You hold my heart, taming an unleashed passion inviting
    peace to this old soul still chasing the fire dancing in the
    sunset.

Virgin

I held an angel in my hands once, she was light as a butterfly.
I could never see beyond her smile and her tears tasted of
fresh rain dripping off new born roses still virgin to the
sunlight.

Fracture: Pen and Ink

Fracture

Someday, love will not fracture my heart, instead it will hold
me with hands soft as the sunrise.
It will untether my wings setting me free to carry in the
wind once again.
Love will touch my lips as well as my heart.
Love will gently pour over me and permeate deep within
every inch of my body, my soul.
Oh how I long to drift in that wind once again.
To feel it run freely across my skin.

The Poem

The poem lives forever in my heart.
I find the words there every time I crawl inside and each
time I come out, I bring you another piece of me.

PART TWO

Grief

Blanket Of Fire

I hear her pale voice crawling through the crystal air.
I feel the fingers of her spirit caressing my sadness to sleep.
She finds me once again beyond my waking breath, blowing
    a gentle whisper against the weight of my throe.
She asks,
    "Will you hold me my love?
    Bring the beat of your heart next to mine."
Suddenly I am everything she needs.
My strength becomes the sunrise on her cold frost covered
    skin, supplicating the feel of my flesh like a fortress
    around her.
I will become her blanket of fire...fighting back her shadows,
    never letting her feel the chill again.
Never letting the edge of darkness near her heart...again.
I will bring her every sunrise, every ounce of my honor.
She will laugh again and she will run free in my soul...
I swear it.
So I wake every day and gather all her favorite flowers, I
    save every smile, every laugh, and all the sunshine my
    heart can carry.
I will bring them to her every time I close my eyes.
I will live every moment she wanted for me, I will carry her
    spirit with every step I take, so that we may share those

moments together...
I swear it.

Crest

The pieces I feel the most.
The corners that carry so much weight.
Pressing against the flat angle ache I caress into the smallest
    grin I can bare.
Rough shards with razor sharp slivers clinging to what the
    wind of my soul feeds them.
A violent verge rolling over my head, hiding the stars and
    the blue blanket canvas of a night sky.
A sky splattered with every sparkle your eyes blessed upon
    me in the passionate silence of my dreams.
The crest of every smile erupting into laughter singing
    throughout this valley filled with so many edges.
The edge of every moment that my fingers almost touched,
    even though it still cuts me every time I try.
Where the wind was kind enough to bless me with the
    gentle breeze of our first kiss, yet it was too much to ask
    for the courage to hold your heart forever.

Slips Further: Pen and Ink

Slips Further

Do you remember her last breath, her last laugh, the first
kiss?
The moment when your heart became hers, feeling her
fingers tickle love from depths you never knew existed.
The times you held her when she cried.
The nights she fell asleep in your arms with the smile you
gave her...
Do you still feel her fingers fade from yours?
Wondering if this is really happening while her last breath
falls and the angels carry her up and away.
Do you still recognize each falling tear every time they
return to the edge of your cheek?
I do...
I feel that cold breeze take over and turn colder as the sun
slips further behind my tears.

Half Moon

And he fell asleep each night whispering the same words,
"we should be doing this together, we should be held in
the silence of our beating hearts forever," like a half
moon never able to crawl to the edge, never able to
reach beyond what he could fully dream of—he fell
asleep every night in the shadow of a light he could
never touch.

Far beyond the tears.

Far past the dirt tired from the salt flooding the earth
beneath him.

Drifting deeper into the layers of memory that prelude the
surface of his pain for her.

He never wanted to be numb, but wanted to feel all the
sharp edges that existed because in each, there might
live a side he had never caressed in fear or in love.

There could be a memory he had yet to drown in, a shadow
to fall in—holding something beyond his fragile fingers,
still tainted in callused breath.

Centuries

I wish had more control over the moments between each
    breath I take.
The centuries living there hold so many hearts.
Sometimes I wish they never held mine.

A Whisper and A Scream

I have always lived by the voice within my heart and I can
  not ignore that.

The voice rises up my throat and crawls over my tongue,
  taking flight from my impassioned lips.

Sometimes as a whisper, other times as a hawk chasing the
  unknowing prey not to hurt, nor to destroy, but to be
  free from what thrusts deep inside.

Once in a while the words carry too much weight, falling off
  my tired tongue back into the swell of my heart and
  where they go from there, only time will tell—or if they
  will have the courage to rise again.

This heart feels like another body, another person
  screaming with joy when love fills every inch of its
  frame, stretching beyond the point of possibility.

It tears, flooding my stomach with an ache before the
  mending clot scabs over with time—one day becoming a
  scar that hangs like a painting on the wall for me to gaze
  upon with pure remembrance.

And now my heart has become a museum, paved like the
  streets of so many cities and lost amongst the clatter of
  feet too shallow to leave a print.

Collectively

It's a beautiful thing to hear nothing.
To be drenched in silence when the only sound you hear are
    memories that fall collectively like rain and all at once
    you hear just your heartbeat and the echo where hers
    would answer your every pulse....your every breath.

Soft Core: Pen and Ink

Soft Core

I want to write of love and how deep we fell into its soft
core.
I want to write of your delicate voice, your laughter and the
sound of your smile erupting.
I want to chase the kisses still lingering in my heart and give
them to you one by one.
Yet when I look inside all I see are pieces of what once was
whole—now torn apart and I can't find all the fragments
to put it back together again.

Coupled

Memories coupled, bearing forth stars shooting from the
    corners of a faded horizon.
Holding hands, jumping across my bleeding heart sky...
    kindled gently into a canvas that clings to the soft
    strokes of laughter, the rough edged screams filled with
    ache, and waves of passion still waiting for more color
    to drown in.
Yet all I find is blue swirled into tired eyes, like a lighthouse
    with no wick trying to show me the way to a peace I
    once found harbored inside the sound of your voice.

Candle

Shadows fall against sunlight in shades we all are familiar
   with, yet grief casts an umbra of so many different
   colors.
Some so dark that not even a candle has a chance to burn.

Grasping

Each decision holds a delicate hope.
Decisions that hold a freedom clinging to a tragic ending.
I cannot see much further than the edge of my heart—
    an edge that falls so far away, far beyond the faint
    echoes still gripping at the rough edges of possibility
    grasping to an endless aspiration that may one day fly so
    far as well.
It's moments like this where I hold my heart in such
    amazement and fear.

Another Heart

I feel so much....

It's so hard not to when every breeze carries a story for me
to breathe in, to listen to as I hold it in my body next to
my heart.

Do you hear it too?

The life of another heart, whispering outside the shadows
we tend to hide our souls in.

Let each breath caress you for a short while, carrying away
what has lingered inside of you for far too long...
darkness.

My Own Spit

I can't seem to see beyond my own darkness.
That light at the end of the tunnel is just laughing at me.
I can't remember a time when the shadow didn't slap me
     cold in the light of day.
Drowning my breath in my own spit.
Oh the subtle echo of defeat.
How long you hang before my thirsty tongue, with promises
     of quench worthy waters that blow away in the mirage
     of hope.
Or is it the jester of my own heart blinding the real fool with
     his own jokes.
I can't tell anymore.
All I can see is a reflection in the light of my tears that are
     still shackled in the hope that you'll save me.
Because I can't seem to save myself.

Burning

I hear the cold wind whistle crawling through the cracks of
    this tired, worn flesh.
I feel it catching up to me.
Edging closer while the dragon inside chases the demon
    living within.
Hold my hand.
Let me feel something beyond the battle raging inside.
Let me feel your fingers wrapped around mine, while I try to
    hold onto the hope I feel burning away.
In your hands I can live for a moment as I once was.
I can run like the light that dances through the wind blowing
    into that small corner of my heart left untouched by the
    darkness.

Droplets

What happened to the days of our tomorrow.
The undying swell of expectations lingering in the essence
of our hearts that never seemed to stop flying.
The constant reassurance existing in each beat of this
blessing we held in our hands.
A miracle in the moment that seems so far away now.
Yet, you still hold mine in your fragile fingers, you hold what
is beyond my sight to see with these thirsty hands.
Hidden, more remote than what my eyes soaked in sorrow
can focus on.
My heart trembles.
Throbbing, lost in the echoes of the deepest ache eagerly
waiting to be unfolded within the blanket of my soul.
Waiting to be taken blindly by your tenderness.
Taken into the cradle that carved out the core of my
essence, molding my wings, setting me free from the
restraints falling in the rearview mirror.
Focusing forward into an uncertainty only touched by your
whispers leaving a trail...leading me toward our dreams.

Sonance: Pen and Ink

Sonance

Maybe it was the sound of my fragile exhale shivering in the
cover of darkness that caught your ear.
A faint lucent reflection, like a lost chord waiting to be
heard.
Wanting to share more than the simple sonance found just
below the surface of my skin.
A pulse tethered to the bone like a leaf never wanting to let
go...only to fall.

Pieces

There are so many pieces of my heart I have never found.
I like to think it's because she is still holding them.
Pieces that she just can't let go of.
And I'm okay with that.
Because I still carry pieces of hers.

Dreams

There's another place I hide them.
Not on that dusty shelf buried from the howling wind
    searching for a fire to feed.
Somewhere beyond the arms of the sun and the fresh smell
    of sulfur swirling after her gentle fingertips.
The wind has carried that away long ago.
Yet, the many scars on that box remain.
A subtle reminder of enduring hope that she found through
    the cobwebs and buried in shadows that she was all too
    familiar with.
A place now where only the morning dew dances and
    memories are held in momentary prisms.
Growing tired of fingers of light and wishing to burn once
    more...
I don't hide them there anymore.

Bare

Last night I stood out in the wind, bare, naked...only dressed
in the fingers of mother nature's breath.
And I swear I felt your whisper touch me, wrapping around
my bones...reaching for more than my heart.
Carving a highway through my veins, seeking a way home.

Pluck

I remember stepping into that dream.
Like a bare foot into a cold stream.
It felt so real, like pain after a fresh cut reeling from a
    retreating thorn pulling gently from ripe skin.
The pluck of that moment still echoes in my thoughts.
Like a ripple traveling across the flat surface of an
    untouched pond.
Sending waves into the once calm waters of a windless soul
    waiting for the storm.
You stole this stale silence thrusting me into love's memory.
All in the exhale of my heart.
In the prison of my dreams seeking the keyhole for a key
    buried beyond my fingers reach.

River

I saw you standing there, the sun shining through your hair
and the scent of your heart drifting deeper into my fear.
Trembling like a lost child.
Whispering, give me your hand.
Let me hold your weary heart next to mine.
Close your eyes and fall into me, I will carry you...
I will lay you in the river of my soul, washing your tears
clean of the pain that weighs you down like an anchor
that never lets go.
I will set you free to spread your wings.
Fly throughout the effervescent sunlight you so desperately
seek.
Quench your thirst for the freedom you and I used to dance
in without fear, filled with love and laughter...
It's still there, waiting in the first kiss of the sun floating into
each new day...
And it still lives in your heart.

My Weakest Breath

Your eyes still say so much.
Pressing through my weakest breath giving into the throe.
They open my heart with such subtle grace.
So skillfully like sendal fingers exposing my deep core.
Setting loose each shadow that follows the descent of my
    tears.
Gripping my scars, clinging to the edge of a precipice I find
    myself lingering from.
Holding onto the ache swelling between my fingers.
Hoping the sunlight you let in will give me strength to hold
    on.
Or maybe let go.

Assumption

When pieces of your heart fall and you don't hear them
collide with the ground.
When they tangle amongst your tears and get lost in the
ripples...you get used to the silence in between.
You stumble into the assumption that maybe they never find
a place to land...yet it takes more time than your heart
can imagine at first.
And some day, when they catch up with the wind pressing
against what's left of your heart, filling the vacant.
It crawls through slowly, like fluid breath drowning all that
once was so still.
Reminding you of the ache that continues to exist on every
edge.

The Echo Of Her Need

I opened her letter today, vulnerably asking for my hand to
    hold hers.
A heartfelt plea on paper where the tear stained ink ran
    behind every word as did the echo of her need.
She loves every kiss I send and feels my arms around her,
    keeping her safe, keeping her near my heart waiting for
    every word born...to fall upon her.
She feels the wind stirring in my soul.
I'm drunk every moment I'm near her.
Yet what she needs far from home is to hold my hand.
To feel the warmth of our fingers locked together.
Squeezing tight in this moment where her heart cries out for
    the feeling of home and the one there waiting for her.
I feel your cry rip through my heart like a rainstorm.
I feel your fingers holding onto the edge of hope wishing it
    weren't so slippery.
Hold on my love, like a lighthouse I will reach for you.
I will find a way through the fog to bring home to you.
I will bring warm breath to your cold lips.
I will bring sunlight to your tired soul.
I will hold your hand fulfilling your heart's most desperate
    plea.

Sadness

She kept kissing the tears that continuously streamed down
my cheeks...
I told her, *"Thank you for sharing my sadness with me."*
She replied, *"I wasn't sharing your sadness with you. I was
tasting the beauty of you letting go."*

Held

I have held many things in my hand.
New born life stretching into its first breath, death robbing
    life from those that should still be breathing.
I've held sunlight and shade, mercy and cruelty.
I've seen those that do not deserve to hold anything other
    than their own fear.
I've held that darkness myself a time or two and cried for
    forgiveness wishing I had not chosen weakness over
    honor.
Though for a long time now I've held the memory of your
    first laugh and your last.
The time I told you, "I love you," in complete heart
    pounding fear, and you brushed aside my small shadow
    answering my words with the same.
And I will forever carry the promise I made to you before
    we parted too soon.
I will never let the shadow return to do so would be to cast a
    shadow on you, and that will never happen.

Etched

The sound of her voice is forever etched into my soul.
Leaving a vivid impression with soft edges dripping slow
    echoes.
Carrying to the surface of my breath changing the way I talk.
Creating a different voice that drowns in the ocean of every
    thought I have.
My heart has fallen into this acoustic groove that no longer
    sings a sad song.
Yet, it rejoices with every beat.
Singing louder and louder so as to never return to the
    shadows and leaving a voice for others to grasp.
Pulling them into the sunlight once again.

Mira

I thought that I was strong.
I thought I was able to endure the shadows, so they would
    never touch your light.
So they would never take away the delicate miracle I saw in
    your eyes.
I found myself lost in that gentle gaze, like a leaf tumbling at
    the mercy of the wind.
And somewhere along the way I realized we were carrying
    each other.
All those long nights I held you in my arms, you were
holding me too.
You were giving me something that I would never
    understand until the moment you graciously let go,
    setting me free.
Pushing your pain aside to comfort mine, showing me the
    true meaning of strength.

Strangers

She never could abstain from sharing the light in her heart.
Regardless of the shadows lingering nearby and nipping at
her heels.
They never scared her from offering it, even to complete
strangers.
She could feel the shadows in others and knew light could
diminish the darkness.
With one word.
One gesture.
And to do so set her free a little bit at a time.

Freedom

She gave me freedom.
The kind my heart had only dreamed of.
I never looked back as the chains fell to the floor.
I never even heard them collide with the shadows I left
  behind.
I outran the echoes as they grasped for another moment of
  misery.
One last chance to feed their desire for company.
And now, I grow thirsty for each new breath I take.

Our Paths: Pen and Ink

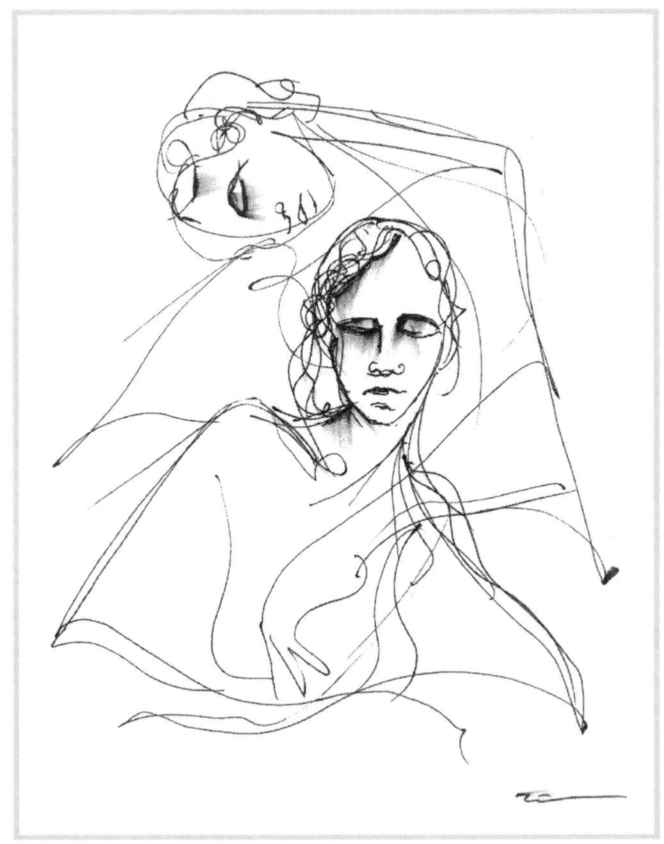

Our Paths

I truly believe we have met before.
And somewhere out there, she is waiting for me to find her
    again.
Somewhere reaching for my hand.
And as many times as our paths have crossed, they will
    again.
Only hoping that this time we will hold each other a little
    while longer than the last.

PART THREE

Life

Clinch

I clinch tight trying to hold onto the light I once let drip
   freely over my bare skin, yet soon realize that all I have
   in my fist is darkness,
So I open my hand slowly—letting go.

Veins

Sometimes we need to scream from more than our hearts.

Sometimes that voice comes to us from beyond an unknown barrier.

Piercing through the small cracks of least resistance, letting us know that we are more than what we see in the mirror.

So much more than what we dress ourselves up with on a daily basis.

Each time we scream, another piece falls.

The veins swell as that wind whistles through the new cracks we create.

Howling into the air like a fresh storm crossing a calm sea, stirring up what we were.

Awakening what we know lies underneath the surface, yet never had the courage to unleash.

That flutter of uncertainty tickling our untamed curiosity bubbling beneath the surface.

Just waiting for a simple pin prick to start the inevitable spew of freedom reaching for a new atmosphere.

Fury

Sometimes in the fury we find pockets of hope.
Sometimes in the silence, fear feels like our only friend.
Between the two it can seem impossible to find balance.
It can be so difficult to find a place where we can hold hope,
    even for a little while.
We unconsciously stumble into one or the other looking
    behind us—instead of finding what unfolds before us.

Blindfold

Loosen up the blindfold hanging over my heart.
For once let me see the scars with my own eyes, rather than
through the ache swelling from underneath.

Tongue

Hold gently to what rests within your hands, don't squeeze
    too tight.
Don't let it slip between your fingers, falling shy of the wind
    screaming from your lips.
Your tongue holds the birth place of all that erupts from
    your heart.

Canvas

Somehow sunlight found a way, dripping casually across the
    canvas of night.
Like a tear rolling slowly over thirsty skin leaving a trail of
    promise.
A pathway to peace that hopefully many will follow.

Dry and Thirsty

I must first sew what I have left open.
What I have ripped with my own fingers blinded by greed
    and hatred.
The need to soften rough edges gone sharp in the shadows
    and left out in the wind grows like a wildfire.
I hear it cling to those little fingers, feeding on this dry and
    thirsty ache for the taste of gentle rain.
Buried somewhere deep inside my heart once held within
    the ocean that reaches deeper than the tears of my
    childhood.
I can feel it with every step I take and I can't outrun it any
    longer.
I now must attempt to mend the unanswered echoes of what
    I have once ignored and must face before I can carry on.

Fingers: Pen and Ink

Fingers

I could hear their voices, reaching for more than my ear.
Gently pouring through a million fingers, extending for the
edge of my heart.
Whispering wisdom like prayers at the altar needing to be
heard.
Hoping we will remember that they need us as much as we
need them to exist.
A balance we fall further from every day looking down into
our own hands.
Instead of lifting our heads up to what is right in front of us.

Honor

Honor is a word used by many and unfortunately held by
few.

A word that feels good when said, yet scares most that bark
its name when the bell rings at the true hour of need.

I am no hero, yet I will run with the fear that fills my blood
rather than run from it.

Give me your hand, I will promise to show the courage that
honor breeds from.

Rising into my fervorous heart ready to face that which
frightens you and desires my protection and undying
affection.

Cage

Have you ever allowed your heart the convenience of
  unaltered expression?
The ability to let flow that which never touches the soul.
That which you never let your mind have the chance to
  amend based on the limitations we live everyday.
The chance to let your heart separate from the tethers of
  life.
It takes great courage to do so and even greater courage to
  give it the chance to be free.
Why do we cage ourselves within the possibility of what we
  can touch.
When deep down we know there is so much more in letting
  go.

Miracle: Pen and Ink

Miracle

Every beat of our hearts is a miracle.

Every single one.

Sometimes we feel them.

Sometimes we hear them, yet many times we go on not
realizing they continue to carry that miracle with each
beat.

We live the next day and the next not fully understanding
how fragile this miracle is.

Until one day when one stops.

We feel that sensation inside, the beating of our heart.

We clinch our chest trying to touch that which is aching so
much.

That portent wonder screaming for us to recognize what we
hold inside each of us—a miracle.

We

We are poets—souls of the word through every breath we
  bleed.
We dip our pens deep in that blood.
We share that with you who choose to read what we feel and
  if you touch it—you can feel it too.
We live in love, death, light and darkness.
We make mistakes and miracles, we fly with the wind and
  we fall face first in the dirt.
We get back up when we fall and if we can't we help each
  other up.
We get lost and found, we get angry and sad, we get
  overwhelmed with joy and bathe in lust that drips from
  the depths of our hearts.
We swim in the sea of our emotions whether it crashes
  against rocky shores or caresses the calm edges of a
  beach we walk holding the hand of our lovers.
We are poets—it's who we are whether we chose it or not—
  and it's truly a blessing as well as a curse to be one
  everyday.

Shortcut

In life there is a path we all must follow.
We may not believe it at first or trust that it is possible.
We think we make our own steps.
Nothing or no one else makes them for us.

We find ourselves diverting in directions filled with passion,
    pain, love and lust.
Screaming in the face of life's intention.
We begin to feel the wheel pulling to the left, all the while
    trying so hard to pull to the right.
Yet somehow we find ourselves back on that path wrapped
    in memories.

I have rested my dizzy head filled with the swell of faith.
I have tried to fight and fuck my way out of that sunlight
    thinking I could find a shortcut through the shadow.
And until she softly kissed my tear soaked cheek I never
    really realized the truth.
That we can fight it into the death of us.
We can plunge into the shadows drawing the warmth from
    our hearts, giving into our demons.
Or we can continue on regardless.
Because life, if we truly believe, has a path for us all.

Like the wind, it will blow soft and swift depending on how hard we fight or flow with it.

Marrow

We hold a history that lives inside us, each one of us.
Buried in the marrow of our souls breathes a lesson we are
losing little by little.
A promise we are obligated to fulfill and share with those
that follow in our footsteps.
That all life matters, people, animals, insects, the wind, the
atmosphere, the oceans and the earth on which we live
everyday.
And no matter how heavy the blanket of fear and hatred that
falls upon our heart—we never let it shatter the
existence of hope.
For in hope lies the future of our souls. We must fight
hatred, not with aggression, but with love.
Love is the only true source of our hearts—we must never
lose that.

Protect

The edges of our hearts are fragile.
Sheltering so much we wish to protect as well as set free.
Everything we let in and unleash creates a scar.

Together

To truly be yourself is to accept all the sides of your heart
and soul, as well as others.
We all have shadows and sunlight.
We all have been victims and villains.
We feel love and loathing. Each of us have healed others as
well as hated.
We open our eyes every morning to a new day regardless of
where the sun shines.
Our toes touch the same earth no matter what country we
live in.
We exist on this planet, all of us together.

Inspiration: Pen and Ink

Inspiration

Inspiration lives and breathes in everything we see and
    touch.
Waiting at the edge of our hearts is the courage to take
    flight, capturing the wind that carries the voice we seek
    to set free.

Saltwater

So many times I have stood on the shore.
Watching the waves crash, listening to the whispers crawl
    through the storm.
My heart pounding , not in fear, but with the weight of the
    pull.
Many times I have felt that sway rock my body back and
    forth as the taste of saltwater falls across my lips.
Staring into the face of the storm.
Teeth grinding, fist clinched...and most days I turn away.
Most days I let the edges harden and my flesh fall numb
    against my pain.
Pain that digs in deep, forming the cracks of my heart.
Cracks form whether you jump in or turn away.
They scar whether we do everything we can or nothing at all
    —and that day I jumped.

Acorn

Today I found a miracle laying before me like the grass or a
    breath of air waiting to cross my lips.
I passed it several times throughout my day and didn't think
    much of it, yet there it was, laying there.
As patient as the dirt beneath my feet, waiting for the rain to
    come and give it a chance at life.

Dilate

There is a moment before each choice we make.
A moment where our soul screams, our eyes dilate, and our
lungs fill with a stormed breath,
That split second before we set free the wild from our
heart's to dance across our tongues is the quietest
moment I have ever known.

Persuasion

Understanding and empathy disappear amongst screams of
  hatred, drowning out the truth we seek.
It misleads our hearts into the shadows of fear, guiding our
  fingers into fists.
Persuasion is fueled by the power of social ignorance.
It pours from the lips of young hearts and misguided leaders
  seeking platforms on every back they can crawl over.
Making flexed statements laced with weak intention to do
  anything except seek out the truth and understanding
  we all desire and deserve.

Skin

What you see on the surface may be run with scars.
It may be riddled with wounds long yet to heal.
Such things do not reflect the depths of what lies below the
     shallow ability of your eyes to see.
If you only look, you will only see to the edge of your fear.
And your fear can only reach so far, like a shadow cast from the
     sun—it is limited in reach.
The light of your heart will carry far beyond such lines.
It is time we looked further than the reflection of our skin
     and found the truth which exists in each of our souls.

Shore

Happiness depends on the ability to see past our fears and
  ideals we leash ourselves with.
See beyond the footprints we make and carve out your own
  existence.
Listen to the sound of your heart and fly further than the
  ripples it creates, before they reach the shore and settle.

Foundation

I try to be a good man.

I try to keep my feet on the ground with my toes pressed
against the cool grass following the beat of my heart,
one step at a time.

Yet I'm tired of standing beneath the podium.

Tired of watching the "good" hand hold down the great
foundation of what we live and fight for...and so many
will and have died for.

I'm tired of watching those that are supposed to protect,
guide and help us turn around after singing promises,
like a church choir only to fall into the shadow of greed
and hate.

This is not what our hearts are made of.

This is not what we desire to pass on to our children and
loved ones.

And as we witness this repeated shadow—woven with
threads of self purpose—claim those that fall short of
their own heart's true purpose.

We must remember, that to continue towards building on
this great foundation of ours, we must do it with love
and integrity, with hope and understanding—not with
the hate and shadows that claim so many hearts by
temptation.

Don't bite into that apple.

Take one step at a time, with our feet on the ground, one day
at a time.

And we must start today, tomorrow and every day after for
the sake of each heart beating and those yet to.

Beyond The Ache

Never let the shadow take your tears, they belong to you.
They are your fear, your hope and if they should fall in the
 darkness that you find yourself drowning in, set them
 on fire.
Follow the flame beyond the shadow, beyond the ache
 clinging to your hope, like shackles wrapped around the
 ankles of your strength, trying to make you believe you
 can't walk, that you can't run—like the wind filled with
 the sunlight of your dreams, because you can and you
 will—if you follow the fire.

Poet's Pain: Pen and Ink

Poet's Pain

Its not easy being a poet.
Its not just words and wonder.
It's not only passion and pleasure found in the depths of a
    soul carved in sunlight kisses that sway like flowers
    with every breath we take.
It's tearing pieces of your heart still soaked in tears.
Using the sharpened edges to etch painful memories you
    wish you didn't have to relive.
Yet need to set free.

About Higherhawk

Higherhawk is a naturalist, a romantic, and a poet. He currently resides in North Carolina, but was raised in the Midwest and lived for many years in Northern California.

Higherhawk spends his spare time hiking and with nature photography.

Thank you for purchasing—*Deciduous*—my debut book of poetry. I truly appreciate you taking the time to read my words. This book was a labor of love, grief and the journey through life. It's not always pleasant, it's not always beautiful, but these words are from the heart.

Social proof is instrumental in helping authors to gain an audience and readership, so if you wouldn't mind, please leave a review at your favorite retailer.

Thank you,
Higherhawk

Made in the USA
Lexington, KY
03 July 2017